DEMCO

TECHNOLOGY: BLUEPRINTS OF THE FUTURE

TECHNOLOGY: BLUEPRINTS OF THE FUTURE

Skyscrapers
Inside and Out

by
Leonard M. Joseph

Illustrations
Leonello Calvetti
Alessandro Bartolozzi, Lorenzo Cecchi, Donato Spedaliere

The Rosen Publishing Group's
PowerPlus Books™
New York

*For my wife, Nancy, and son, Jeffrey, who
always support me and share my enthusiasm for understanding the world around us*

Published in 2002 in North America
by The Rosen Publishing Group, Inc., New York

First Edition

Book Design:
Andrea Dué s.r.l. Florence, Italy

Illustrations:
Alessandro Bartolozzi, Leonello Calvetti, Lorenzo Cecchi, Donato Spedaliere
3D models: Luca Massini

Editor and Photo Researcher:
Joanne Randolph

Researcher:
Georgene Poulakidas

Library of Congress Cataloging-in-Publication Data

Joseph, Leonard M.
Skyscrapers : inside and out / by Leonard M. Joseph. — 1st ed.
p. cm. — (Technology—blueprints of the future)
Includes bibliographical references and index.
ISBN 0-8239-6109-5 (library binding)
1. Skyscrapers—Juvenile literature. [1. Skyscrapers.] I. Title. II. Series.
TH9445.T18 J67 2002
720'.483--dc21
2001001115
Manufactured in Italy by Eurolitho S.p.A., Milan

Contents

The Language of Skyscrapers

We're surrounded by buildings, but some seem truly special. You may always feel drawn to an alcove in your home with a window seat that happens to be just the right height. You may have run your hands over lovingly carved woodwork. Some buildings stick in one's memory. City Hall may be fronted with awe-inspiring columns. The museum may have a grand interior space where daylight pours down on a sculpture, etching shadows in it. A skyline crowded with tall buildings is, to many of us, an inspiring symbol of today's large, modern cities.

Such special buildings and places do not happen by accident. We say a building was designed, because an architect made a building special by its shape, its position, or by the use of color or pattern. Artistic design goes beyond strict necessity: a stained-glass window, dappled with color, may not keep out the rain any better than a plain window does, but it is far more pleasing.

Engineers are also thought to be designers, even though their way of designing is different from that of architects. To an engineer, a beautiful skyscraper looks lighter than it is, or it neatly tucks all its pipes and electrical systems into unusually small spaces.

Architects and engineers, however, are only two kinds of experts out of the hundreds it can take to determine a skyscraper's form and the thousands it can take to build one. The beauty of a great skyscraper comes from resolving seemingly contradictory problems. It must be sturdy, yet it must be economical to build; it must be beautiful,

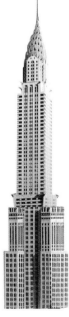

| SEAGRAM BUILDING New York USA 1959 525 feet (160 m) | MESSETURM Frankfurt, Germany 1990 843 feet (257 m) | TRANSAMERICA PYRAMID San Francisco USA 1972 853 feet (260 m) | CITICORP CENTER New York USA 1977 915 feet (279 m) | OUB BUILDING Singapore 1986 919 feet (280 m) | LANDMARK TOWER Yokohama Japan 1993 971 feet (296 m) | LIBRARY TOWER Los Angeles USA 1989 1,018 feet (310 m) | CHRYSLER BUILDING New York USA 1930 1,046 feet (319 m) |

but it must also be suitable for use by thousands of people over many decades. It must accommodate all kinds of technology, from elevators and escalators to ducts and fans for heating and cooling to cables and switches for computers and telephones. Indeed, some of the most beautiful skyscrapers have been made to show off the complex technologies that made them possible.

As shown in the book you are about to read, the imaginations of the architect and engineer are tempered by the concerns of owners, builders, banks, and local officials. Sometimes the building designers can think of a way to turn the many restrictions that apply to their projects into something awe-inspiring. Over twelve decades they have refined the way tall buildings are designed, learning to build structures we all recognize, like the Chrysler Building and the Empire State Building in New York, or the Petronas Towers in Malaysia. Skyscrapers have become the symbols of many American cities, and indeed, of cities throughout the world.

The architecture of a building can "speak" about how the building was made and how it works. It can embody an owner's aspirations and it can help to make a city memorable. I hope this book will help you look at skyscrapers with new eyes, perhaps allowing you to "read" buildings in the language they speak—design.

James S. Russell
Editor at Large
Architectural Record
New York

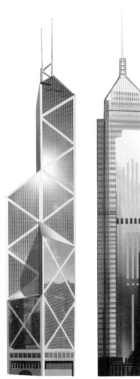

BANK OF CHINA	CENTRAL PLAZA	EMPIRE STATE BUILDING	WORLD TRADE CENTER	SEARS TOWER	PETRONAS TOWERS
Hong Kong	Hong Kong	New York	New York	Chicago	Kuala Lumpur
1989	1992	USA 1931	USA 1972	USA 1974	Malaysia 1998
1,209 feet (369 m)	1,227 feet (374 m)	1,252 feet (382 m)	1,368 feet (417 m)	1,450 feet (442 m)	1,483 feet (452 m)

What Is a Skyscraper?

We often think of skyscrapers when we think of cities. One glance at a postcard and we know if it's from New York, Chicago, Paris, or Shanghai, because modern cities are defined by their skyscrapers. Yet these buildings have been around for only a century. What are skyscrapers, anyway? Why are they built? Who builds them? How are they built? What keeps them standing? Who uses them? To answer these questions, let's look at six of the tallest and best-known skyscrapers from different times and in different countries:

- The Empire State Building opened in 1931 in New York City and stands 1,252 feet (382 m) tall.
- The World Trade Center twin towers were completed in 1972 in New York City. The taller one was 1,368 feet (417 m) high.
- Sears Tower, completed in 1974 in Chicago, Illinois, is 1,450 feet (442 m) tall.
- The Bank of China Building was completed in 1989 in Hong Kong. It stands 1,209 feet (369 m) tallß.
- The Jin Mao Tower, completed in 1998 in Shanghai, China, stands 1,380 feet (421 m) tall.
- The Petronas Towers were completed 1998 in Kuala Lumpur, Malaysia. Each of the twin towers is 1,483 feet (452 m) tall.

Changing times led to changing ways of designing and building skyscrapers. Read on and you'll know skyscrapers inside and out!

• • • • • • • • • • •

Many skyscraper definitions tell more about the people definign skyscrapers than about the buildings themselves. From real estate agents to firefighters to mechanical engineers, every person has a unique perspective on what makes a building a skyscraper.

The general public might say, "A skyscraper is something really tall." Is height enough to qualify a building as a skyscraper? The 404-foot (123-m) steeple of

The cathedral in Ulm, Germany, the pyramids of Giza, Egypt, and the Eiffel Tower, though tall, are not skyscrapers.

Salisbury Cathedral in England has stood since 1315, but it's not a skyscraper. The Eiffel Tower in Paris is even taller, at 984 feet (300 m), but it's a monument, not a skyscraper. Skyscrapers must be buildings, with multiple floors enclosed within walls and a roof.

Structural engineers might say, "Skyscrapers are tall, slender buildings that require special attention to their structural building frames to provide lateral strength and stiffness against wind." Both height and slenderness are important factors to consider, since narrow buildings are easier to topple. The Pyramids are tall, but they're not skyscrapers!

Architects may choose a practical or an artistic definition. In 1900, Cass Gilbert, a well-known architect of beautiful, monumental buildings, said that a skyscraper was "a machine that makes the land pay." A skyscraper uses much more vertical space, or air space, than it does space on the ground, by stacking floors on top of each other. By renting the space in all of those floors, the buiding's owner can make money even where land is very expensive. Cesar Pelli, the architect of the Petronas Towers in Malaysia, agrees that tall buildings must be economically attractive to exist, but he says that "high rise" can describe any tall building, but only "skyscrapers" have forms that direct the viewer's eyes up towards the heavens.

The Trump Tower in Manhattan.

Opposite:
The skylines of lower Manhattan and Hong Kong.

Why Build Skyscrapers?

Long ago, people climbed scattered trees in the grassy African savanna for safety. We still like height today, whether we are sitting on a hill or are perched in a tree house. Height has also been related to power. For example, loyal subjects have always bowed before kings and queens on thrones.

It is no surprise that building tall was a goal of many people interested in security or in showing their power. Ancient pyramids and mausoleums, or tombs, demonstrated this urge in memorials for the dead. Castles and towers reflected it for the living. A famous example of "tower power" is the Italian town of San Gimignano, where wealthy families competed in the 1200s by building narrow towers up to 177 feet (54 m) high. Eventually there were seventy-two towers darkening the narrow streets with their shadows. Most of the towers have since been removed, but the remaining fourteen look like a mini-Manhattan, New York, skyline in the Italian hills.

Nevertheless, tall castles, pyramids, and steeples don't qualify as skyscrapers. Unlike all of these structures, skyscrapers are built to make money by fitting as much rentable space as possible on the least amount of land. Building a successful skyscraper means making decisions about rents and costs, taking large loans, meeting short time schedules, and using modern technology. For a skyscraper to be successful, rents must be greater than payments on loans for buying the land, the cost of construction, and the cost of running and maintaining the building. Predicting rental rates for a future skyscraper is one of a developer's toughest tasks.

Generally, skyscrapers are built in city locations on expensive land, to provide spaces in which people can conveniently, comfortably, and efficiently live or work. Building standards depend on how the skyscrapers will be used—as shops, offices, or apartments—and also on the local laws, culture, history, and climate. Floor layouts for apartments and hotels certainly differ from those for offices. Even for the same use, skyscraper floors in New York City differ from those in Chicago, Berlin, or Hong Kong. Developers and architects shape buildings to suit regional needs.

The San Gimignano skyline

Left: Even in medieval Italy people wanted to live in tall buildings. This is a tower in Florence, Italy.

Right and above: In the Marina Towers in Chicago, the lower parking garage levels have different floor plans from the upper apartments levels.

Facing page, above: A typical Tuscan tower from the thirteenth century.

Getting Inside: How Do Skyscrapers Work?

A skyscraper is really a collection of building systems, designed and built by specialized teams of people. Some of the systems keep the building standing upright. Some move occupants up and down. Some systems provide safety, and others keep the occupants comfortable.

STARTING THE PROCESS

People who want a building to be built for them form an ownership group, called the owner. Successful owners have good relationships with the city government, the local real estate community, and financing sources.

Owners' personalities can affect a building's design. For example, John J. Raskob, founder of General Motors, was a part owner of the Empire State Building (ESB). As a fierce competitor of fellow automaker Walter Chrysler, Raskob made sure that the ESB was built 200 feet (61 m) taller than the Chrysler Building, which had been completed a year earlier!

For the owner of the Jin Mao Building in Shanghai, design was based on the Chinese lucky number eight. The building rises in sections like a pagoda. Each section is set back 0.8 meter (2.6 feet) from the one below. The lowest section has sixteen (8 x 2 = 16) floors. The number of floors in upper sections reduces by two (1/8 x 8 x 2 = 2) floors at a time until reaching a section with eight floors. Sections above that point reduce by one (1/8 x 8 = 1) floor at a time. Counting by sections, the total number of floors above the ground is eighty-eight (16 + 14 + 12 + 10 + 8 +7 +6 + 5 + 4 + 3 + 2 + 1 = 88). The building's dedication was set for the lucky date 8/28/98.

The owner may choose to hire a firm that has expertise, or special knowledge, in hiring and guiding the professionals who design buildings and the contractors who build them. These people are called developers. They manage the business end of the building process, but they don't intend to have long-term ownership.

ASSEMBLING AND CLEARING THE SITE

The developer may assist in acquiring new land. This can be tricky when a large piece of land is needed. In older cities the land may have many different landowners, each holding a small parcel, or portion of the land. The developer buys parcels while keeping the project secret. If landowners learn that their land is being bought for a large project, they can demand higher prices and the last few pieces of land can be expensive indeed. Of course, bargaining can go both ways. Look around any city and you'll see odd little buildings tucked into sides or rears of skyscrapers, where the last "holdout" asked too much money for their land and was passed by.

Skyscrapers are usually built in cities, where land has already been developed. The owner often pays a demolition contractor to remove the old buildings and allows the contractor the "salvage rights" to resell whatever items of value are found. When other buildings are nearby, demolition is a slow, brick-by-brick process. Scaffolding, or a temporary roof, is built over sidewalks around the site to protect people from falling objects. When a whole block of buildings is to be demolished, controlled implosion may be used. The old buildings are stripped of salvage items and are scientifically weakened by chopping holes in walls and notches in beams and columns. Hundreds of small explosives set in the holes and notches are wired to a master board. Explosions are timed so that the center of the building falls first, pulling outer walls inward so no debris lands outside the site. Bulldozers and cutting torches are needed to remove the mountain of debris, but implosion is still a faster, safer, and cheaper process than the brick by brick method.

Left: The Jin Mao Tower in Shanghai was designed with the Chinese lucky number 8 in mind.

Top Right: A building is being imploded to make way for a bigger building.

Bottom Right: A huge crane sits in the center of a construction site.

Starting the Design

Before the architects are hired, the owner or developer already has planned what rents can be charged and how much floor space should be built on the site. The architects use those abstract numbers to plan realistic, practical building shapes.

First, the floor layouts must meet the needs of the people using the building, called the tenants. Before fluorescent lighting and air conditioning, offices could not be too far from windows, the main sources of light and air. In the Empire State Building, architects allowed only 28 feet (8.5 m) from window to interior corridor wall, or core. In Europe, building codes require similar measurements. In North America, most new office buildings have 40 to 50 feet (12.2 to15.2 m) from window to core. In residential buildings, though, the distance to windows must be much shorter, as no one wants to live in long, narrow, dark rooms.

The second requirement is an efficient building core. The core is the "heart" of a building where elevators, exit stairs, mechanical piping, and airshafts are located. In offices it also holds bathrooms and service areas. The core area must be as small as possible, usually taking up just 25% to 30% of the total building space, because tentants don't consider it usable space.

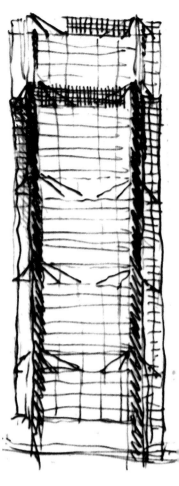

Above: Study sketch for the Hong Kong and Shanghai Bank in Hong Kong

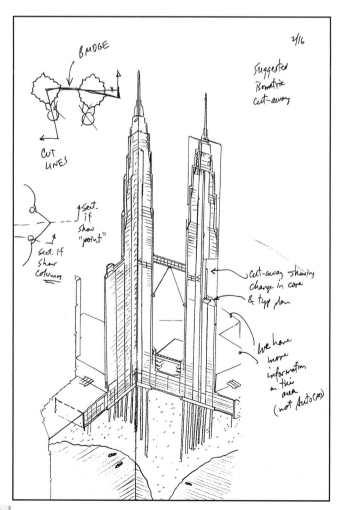

The third requirement is a minimum story height. This depends on what the space will be used for and who the owner wants as tenants. For apartments, typical ceiling height is 8 feet (2.4 m). Total story height can be less than 9 feet (2.7 m). Office buildings have larger story heights to make room for special computer flooring, movable air ducts, and other requirements. The World Trade Center used 12 feet (3.7 m) per story. Today, buildings require story heights of at least 13.5 feet (41 m). These taller stories increase building costs.

Right, top: A bird's-eye view plan of a Petronas Tower upper floor shows elevators and stairs in the central core.

Left: A rough cutaway sketch of the Petronas Towers. Such a drawing would have been adjusted and refined as the construction process got under way.

The fourth requirement is to meet local zoning and building code requirements. One example of these requirements is the total building area allowed. In New York, space is set by the floor area ratio, or FAR. If a FAR of 15 is allowed, usable space in the building cannot be more than 15 times the land area of the property. An owner who wants more usable space can include a plaza or a public space. That increases the FAR to 18. Sometimes an owner can build taller buildings by buying "air rights" from nearby, shorter buildings that did not use up all of their FAR, too.

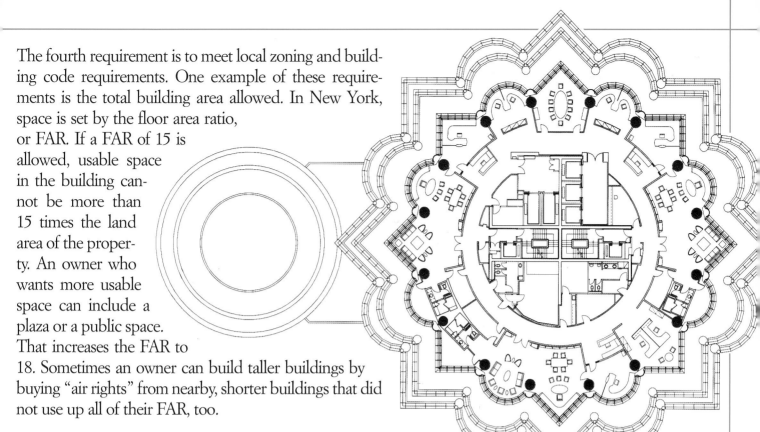

The fifth requirement is an appropriate number of stories. The number of stories affects the number of elevators needed, the construction cost and schedule, and the shape of the building. Starting with an estimated core size and a preferred distance from core to window, the architect can calculate the space on a typical floor. The architect divides the total building area allowed by the typical floor size to estimate the number of stories possible.

The sixth architectural design requirement is fire safety. Being fire safe does not mean a building is totally fireproof, though. It means that the building will contain the spread of flames, heat, and smoke until firefighters put out the blaze. Floor slabs and walls are specially constructed to contain fire for a certain number of hours. Steel softens and loses strength when hot. To keep steel below 1,000°F (538°C), beams and columns are covered with fireproofing or concrete. Sprinklers improve protection by quickly drenching and cooling fires. Fans can be used to vent smoke, and exit stairs allow people to evacuate when necessary.

Below: This floor plan of Petronas Towers at Level 22 is tilted to show an inside view. It has steel beams (yellow lines) running between the concrete core walls (red) and concrete beams connecting concrete perimeter columns (red). The bustle, or smaller circle, shown provides extra space at lower floors.

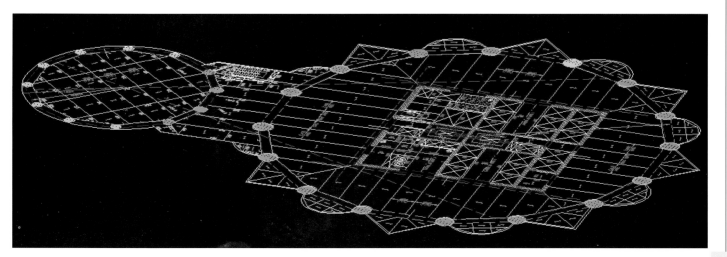

From Design to Construction

In building a skyscraper, the architects, engineers, and consultants do their work first. They use their knowledge and experience, scientific calculations, code requirements, and the advice of specialists to plan what will be needed in the building. This is called the design phase. By the end of the design phase, they have prepared a set of drawings that show what should be included in the completed building to make it stand up safely and function properly. Fifty years ago these drawings were white lines on blue paper, called blueprints; today the drawings are computer plots or photocopies. They also prepare specifications, or books that describe in words the exact requirements for the materials and equipment to be included in the completed building.

The next step is to hire a contractor, or construction firm. Usually the owner selects one firm to be the general contractor, or GC. The GC agrees on a price to provide a building that matches the drawings and specifications and to follow a particular construction schedule, or timetable. On the Petronas Towers, developer KLCC chose two different GCs: a team led by Japanese contractor Hazama for Tower One and a team led by Korean contractor Samsung for Tower Two. This introduced a bit of healthy competition and, because "two heads are better than one," led to creative solutions to construction problems.

The third step is construction. The general contractor figures out what work needs to be done, what order of tasks to follow, and what special assistance is needed from subcontractors. Subcontractors may include fabricators who cut and prepare steel beams and columns, erectors who lift and assemble steel pieces, concrete suppliers, plumbers, electricians, sheet metal fabricators (or "tin knockers"), painters, and hundreds of other specialists.

Above: This model of the World Trade Center might have been used in wind tunnel tests, or to attract investors and tenants.

Left: The top of the Petronas Tower structure uses stainless steel for both the skeleton and the skin, or covering. It covers the window-washing cranes.

Right: The "mooring mast" of the Empire State Building, a steel frame covered with cast aluminum panels, was shown in the original blueprints. It didn't really moor, or attach, blimps. It has proved handy for supporting antennas, though! The little platforms at the base of the mast protect the antennas below from falling ice.

Getting Down: Skyscraper Foundations and Basements

The portions of the building below ground level, or grade, provide basement space and spread the building's weight so that it does not sink into the earth. Foundations are designed to work with super-structure framing, which is the part of the building above ground.

The foundation can make up 5% to 10% of a building's cost, so the owner wants early information on what kind of foundation will be needed. The ground can hold many surprises. A flat racetrack site for the Petronas Towers concealed a deep, soil-filled, *V*-shaped ravine under the area where the two towers were to be built. In the original plans, one edge of each tower would have been sitting on rock, and the other edge would have been sitting on soil 500 feet (150 m) thick. The thick soil would have settled more than the rock. The difference in settlement would have caused the towers to tilt. After this condition was discovered, the plan was changed. Each building location was shifted 165 feet (50 m) farther back from the street. They now sit only on soil, not on rock.

Other sites can have different surprises. Soil may hold hazardous chemicals or historic artifacts. In New York, builders have found old, unmarked graveyards and buried ships. In Mexico City, subway construction exposed Aztec pyramids. London sites have included Roman ruins. You never know what will turn up once you start digging!

Skyscrapers usually have big basements for parking garages, mechanical rooms, shopping areas, and subway station connections. Where the basement is deep, the water table, or natural level of groundwater, may be above the bottom of the excavation. Digging these large holes requires special construction and excavation methods. Slurry wall construction was developed in Europe and was used for all the buildings discussed in this book except the Empire State Building. Slurry walls create a watertight enclosure, or "bathtub," around the future basement. Once a watertight enclosure is created, the excavation subcontractor digs out the dirt within the enclosure. As digging proceeds, the walls need tiebacks to keep them from falling into the hole. Much later when columns and floor slabs are built to complete the basement, the basement floors will hold back the walls. At that time the tiebacks will be released.

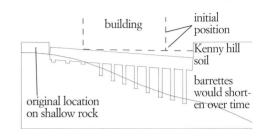

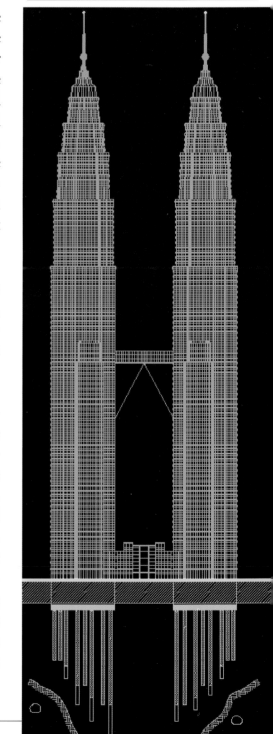

When a large hole is dug at a construction site, a big question is what to do with all the dirt. At the Petronas Towers, the soil was used to create hills for a park on the property. At the World Trade Center, it was dumped right next door to extend the city shoreline. The soil created 23 acres (9.3 ha) of new land worth $90 million. What a deal, considering how much it would have cost to haul away the soil!

Underground conditions can vary widely. Different conditions require different foundations with different costs. Those costs are considered by owners planning to build, as shown by the skyline of Manhattan, New York. Skyscrapers occur in the Wall Street area and in Midtown, where excellent rock is close to the surface. In other areas of Manhattan where rock is farther underground, tall buildings are rare.

Opposite, top: The location of the Petronas Towers was shifted to avoid having one end of the mat, or foundation, on rock and the other on long piles. This could have led to tilting, as shown here.

Opposite, bottom: Under the Petronas Towers, long "fingers," or barrettes, of concrete gradually spread the building weight into the soil, rather than touching the rock far below.

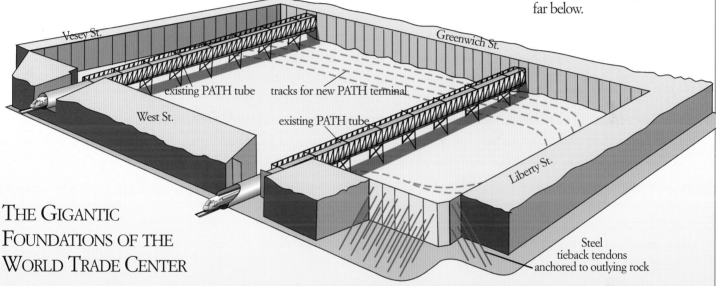

Vesey St.
Greenwich St.
existing PATH tube
tracks for new PATH terminal
West St.
existing PATH tube
Liberty St.
Steel tieback tendons anchored to outlying rock

THE GIGANTIC FOUNDATIONS OF THE WORLD TRADE CENTER

A foundation wall built as a "slurry wall" starts with a hole dug in the soil. To hold it open, the hole is filled with a watery clay called slurry.

The next step is to lower steel reinforcing bars into the hole to make a "rebar cage." The dark triangles are special boxes where tiebacks will later be attached to hold the wall back against the soil.

Finally, a funnel and a long pipe direct concrete to fill the hole from bottom up, lifting slurry out while keeping the concrete from becoming diluted and weakened. This is called the tremie method.

THE EXCAVATION JOB
The slurry wall formed a watertight "bathtub" around the 3,100-foot (944.8-m), rectangular concrete basement perimeter wall of one of the World Trade Center towers. Here more than 1 million cubic yards (750,000 m³) of land were excavated for the 110-story twin towers to soar from bedrock. The exposed tubes enclosed the PATH commuter railroad, which continued operating as usual during construction. The dotted lines indicate tracks for a new PATH terminal. Diagonal lines on the Liberty Street corner show a number of the steel tendons, or tiebacks, used to anchor wall to the outlying rock.

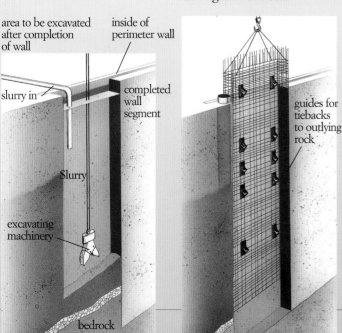

area to be excavated after completion of wall
inside of perimeter wall
slurry in
completed wall segment
Slurry
excavating machinery
bedrock

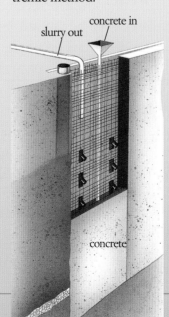

guides for tiebacks to outlying rock
concrete in
slurry out
concrete

Looking Up: Structural Framing

The structural frame, or skeleton, of a skyscraper must be strong and stiff for vertical, downward loads from building weight and occupants, and for lateral, or sideways, loads from wind and earthquakes. The weights of common building materials are well known, so downward loads are relatively easy to figure out. Wind and earthquake conditions are more complicated.

Wind loads cause overturning or tipping forces that try to topple awhole building. Wind also causes shear forces, where one floor tries to slide sideways over another. A wind tunnel is often used to determine the wind forces that could occur during severe storms. A wind tunnel is a long, narrow room with a large fan at one end to push air through it. A scale model of the planned skyscraper, along with nearby buildings, is attached to a large turntable in the floor for testing wind from different directions. Often the scale is 1 to 400, so a 1,200-foot-tall (366-m-tall) building will have a 3-foot-tall (1-m-tall) model.

Different models are used for four different types of wind-tunnel tests. A rigid model is used for the force-balance test. A sensitive scale under the wind tunnel floor measures shear and overturning forces. An aeroelastic model has hinges and springs so it can "wiggle" in the wind as a slender, real building would. A pressure-tap model has 400 thin, plastic tubes running from holes on the model faces, or fronts, to tiny pressure gauges. Pressure information is used to determine window-glass thickness and to design the outside walls. A pedestrian-level wind model tests for gusty winds on sidewalks around the building, because a skyscraper may direct faster winds from higher altitudes down to the ground.

In a successful skyscraper, the building will certainly sway a bit in windy weather, but the tenants should not be uncomfortable. Designers also use something

Above: Wind whistling between towers and around corners creates forces on tall buildings.

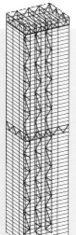

In a two-way moment frame, rigid joints between beams and columns create a "jungle gym."

For taller buildings, moment frame column spacing must be smaller to provide stiffness.

Diagonal bracing between elevators creates the vertical trusses of a braced core. This provides stiffness economically.

Hat trusses and belt trusses link the core and exterior columns to add stiffness for taller buildings.

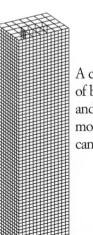

A combination of braced core and perimeter moment frame can also work.

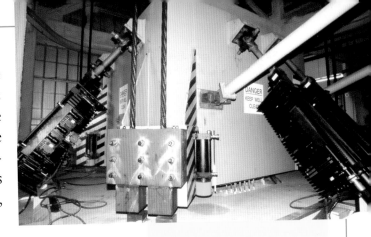

called damping to reduce building sway. It is related to the materials and construction of the building frame. Concrete structures have more damping than steel ones. Sometimes damping is added to buildings to improve comfort. The World Trade Center has 20,000 small dampers that have soft plastic sandwiched between steel plates. In other buildings, a giant steel or concrete block, weighing 400 tons (362.9 t) or more, swings back and forth in a rooftop room, pushing a shock absorber that provides damping.

Strength and stiffness in the frame are also important for safety in earthquakes. Because of their ability to sway or be somewhat flexible, tall buildings are less affected by earthquakes than are short, stiff buildings. Even so, a skyscraper's frame must be stiff enough to hold its shape so the columns stay near vertical. Otherwise whole stories could collapse. Also, the building frame must have the ability to absorb large forces and movements without breaking. Otherwise pieces of the frame could break before an earthquake ends.

In a Tuned Mass Damper (TMD), the mass can swing left to right and front to back, but the gray rods keep it from twisting. The yellow-and-black cylinder is a jack that lifts the weight off the hanging cables when they need to be replaced, and that locks the mass from swinging if necessary. Visible beneath the mass is a "comb" of steel teeth that can gently stop the mass if it swings too far. TMDs should be located where building sway is the greatest. This TMD room is the glass-faced penthouse atop 50-story Chifley Tower. Chifley Tower is part of the distinctive skyline of Sydney, Australia.

Above: The Hong Kong and Shanghai Bank's frames.

When perimeter columns can be closely spaced, a "perimeter tube frame" like the World Trade Center has on the outside do all the work, so no braces are needed in the core.

Diagonal braces around the outside can also provide stiffness without closely spaced columns. The John Hancock Tower in Chicago uses this approach.

When even more stiffness is needed, "bundled tubes" of moment frames with closely spaced columns can do the job. The Sears Towers, in Chicago, uses this approach.

A Skyscraper's Skin

THE CURTAIN WALL

Once the frame is built, curtain walls, or the building's "skin," need to be put up. Skyscrapers must be sealed against high winds and rain, while allowing for building movements. The architect, curtain wall consultant, and testing laboratory all work together to develop a system that has beauty, works reliably, is practical to fabricate, and is easy to install and maintain.

In older skyscrapers, a brick wall backup was used to support a facing, like the Indiana limestone of the Empire State Building. The Empire State Building curtain wall has 10 million bricks, but its design of vertical strips permitted fast construction. A strip of stone alternates with an open strip later filled with windows and aluminum panels. Stainless steel strips close the joint between stone and window.

Newer curtain walls can use glass panes held by aluminum frames. Spandrel panels, or the glass panels covering spandrel beams (the beams along the outside of a building), are blanked out and insulated from behind. Rubber strips keep out wind and water. Each curtain wall design is tested in full-size mock-ups. A three-story-high, 30-foot-wide (9-m-wide) wall is built across the open face of a giant box at an open-air laboratory. Some air is pumped out of the box to create a slight vacuum effect, which can happen in a building. Then spray nozzles and a giant fan (one lab uses a World War II fighter plane engine and propeller) blow water and wind on the wall, like a hurricane, to check for leaks.

Recently, to speed construction, curtain walls have been "unitized." That is, the glass spandrel panels and the surrounding frame are assembled and sealed in the factory to form a larger panel. Joints between neighboring panels are "tongue and groove," where a rib, or tongue, along the edge of one panel slides into a long groove along the edge of its neighbor. Rubber seals and built-in gutters keep leaks from entering a building. On the Petronas Towers, each panel is 4.6 feet (1.4 m) wide by 13.1 feet (4 m) high and has a stainless steel spandrel panel and three lines of stainless steel sunshades.

For safety, modern curtain walls are designed to be installed from inside a building. Small panels, like those on the Petronas Towers and the World Trade Center, brought up on elevators or hoists and are poked out between columns, swung into position, nested to adjacent panels, and hooked to the building. Heavy panels may be carried by a Chicago boom, a human-sized crane strapped to a column on a higher floor.

Below: This is a drawing of the hole at the top of the Shanghai World Financial Center. Notice the steel columns and beams and the glass panels that make up the "skin."

Right: The cutaway drawing shows an exterior wall column of the World Trade Center. Note the aluminum cover and fire-proofing material around the column.

Far right: The World Trade Center wall was erected in premade panels, with vertical columns already welded to horizontal spandrels. Here a 22-ton (20-t) unit, 36 feet (11 m) high and 10 feet (3 m) wide, is being swung into place.

interior wall

steel
column

aluminum
column
cover

fireproofing

stainless steel window-washing track

THE WORLD TRADE CENTER
EXTERIOR WALL COLUMN

Interiors

After the floor is enclosed by a curtain wall, fire-rated walls are built around elevators and airshafts. Walls made of gypsum sheet rock, or drywall, are screwed to studs, or light vertical pieces made of thin steel sheets bent into *C* shapes. Masons build walls of brick or special concrete chunks called cinder blocks. When everything is enclosed and dry, electricians install the transformers, cables, conduits, bus bars, building controls, lights, and outlets.

Underneath the floor above, air ducts, pipes for sprinklers, wiring for ceiling lights, and other mechanical items are installed in locations and sequences that are worked out before installation to avoid conflicts. Once they are in place, the ceiling installer uses special wires hanging from the slab and beams above to attach the ceiling grid and to install ceiling tiles.

Raised floors may be part of the original building or may be put in later. To complete the space, the casework and millwork subcontractor brings in doors and fixed furniture; iron mongers, or locksmiths, attach door hardware; plumbers set fixtures; masons place tiles; signage contractors install signs; and painters finish it all off.

After the basic building design is complete, tenants will begin planning their own spaces. Their interior designers must check with the owner, the architect, and the engineers to be sure the planned spaces meet code requirements and won't damage the building.

Opposite: The columns in the upper floors of the Petronas Towers are set back, allowing tapering at the building's top that reduces exposure to high-altitude winds.

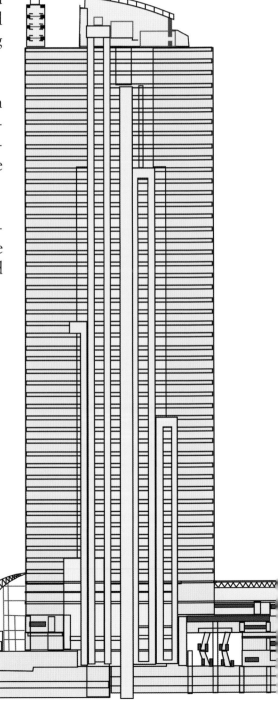

Left:
The atrium in the Bay-Adelaide Centre, in Toronto, Canada, is an example of a finished interior.

Right: This cross-section of the Bay-Adelaide Centre shows the variety of different spaces included in modern skyscraper designs.

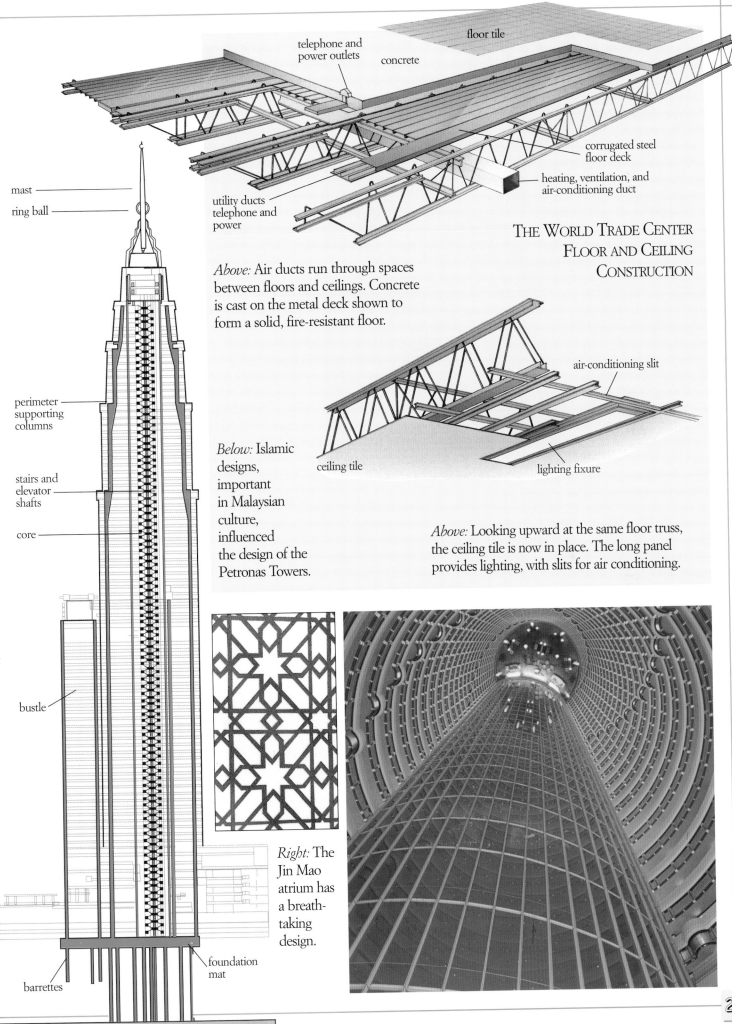

floor tile

telephone and
power outlets

concrete

mast

ring ball

corrugated steel
floor deck

heating, ventilation, and
air-conditioning duct

utility ducts
telephone and
power

THE WORLD TRADE CENTER
FLOOR AND CEILING
CONSTRUCTION

perimeter
supporting
columns

Above: Air ducts run through spaces
between floors and ceilings. Concrete
is cast on the metal deck shown to
form a solid, fire-resistant floor.

air-conditioning slit

stairs and
elevator
shafts

core

ceiling tile

lighting fixture

Below: Islamic
designs,
important
in Malaysian
culture,
influenced
the design of the
Petronas Towers.

Above: Looking upward at the same floor truss,
the ceiling tile is now in place. The long panel
provides lighting, with slits for air conditioning.

bustle

Right: The
Jin Mao
atrium has
a breath-
taking
design.

foundation
mat

barrettes

New York's Most Famous

THE EMPIRE STATE BUILDING

The Empire State Building is perhaps one of the most famous skyscrapers. What did it take to build this well-known giant? For strength, The ESB was built with crossing moment frames and stiff X-braces hidden within some walls. Even so, it requires 60,000 tons (54,400 t) of steel to support 2.1 million square feet (195,000 m²) of floor space, or 57 pounds of steel per square foot (280 kg/m²) of floor. At least four cranes were used to lift, place, and rivet the steel together.

However, the whole building was completed incredibly quickly, in just over one year. At times a whole floor was built in a day, thanks to the 3,500 workers who were on-site at the same time. The results were solid. On foggy July 28, 1945, an Air Force B-25 bomber crashed into the seventy-ninth floor. Twelve people died and parts of the plane went clear through the building, but the structural frame stayed intact.

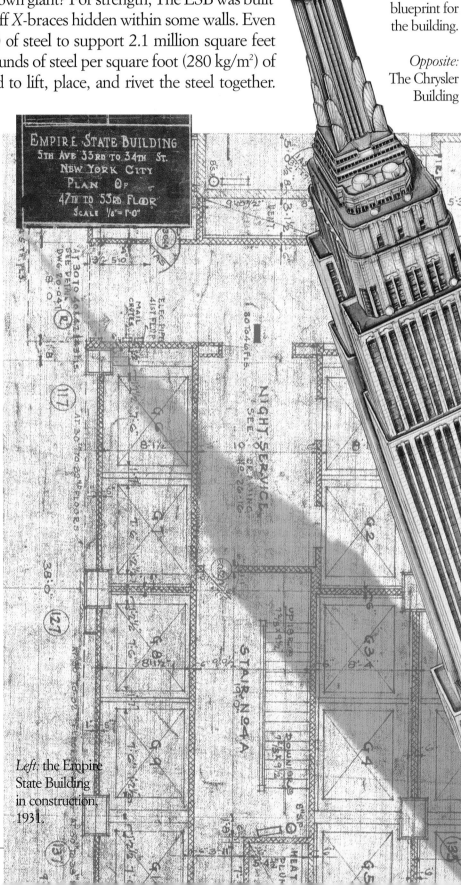

Below: The Empire State Building and a blueprint for the building.

Opposite: The Chrysler Building

EMPIRE STATE BUILDING
5TH AVE 33RD TO 34TH ST.
NEW YORK CITY
PLAN OF
47TH TO 53RD FLOOR
SCALE ⅛"=1'-0"

Left: the Empire State Building in construction, 1931.

More than 1,000 feet (304 m) above the ground without protection, these men are helping to build the Empire State Building.

THE CHRYSLER BUILDING

The Chrysler Building is another of New York's most famous buildings. The owner, Walter Chrysler of Chrysler Motors, wanted ". . . a bold structure declaring the glories of the modern age."

The Chrysler Building was built in the middle of a skyscraper war, in which architects everywhere were trying to build the world's tallest building. William van Alen, the architect of the Chrysler Building, secretly had the 180-foot (55-m) needle constructed in five sections, inside the building's upper floors. At the last minute, the needle was assembled and put up in just 90 minutes. This allowed the Chrysler to claim the title of tallest building in the world by 119 feet (36 m). If the ploy had been known, other buildings being constructed at the time would probably have had design changes to seize the title.

The World Trade Center and Sears Tower

THE WORLD TRADE CENTER

The World Trade Center towers, which were tragically felled in a terrorist attack on September 11, 2001, were another famous New York skyscraper team. Built in 1972, the twin tower frames differed from the Empire State Building. Each tower resisted wind loads using only its perimeter, or outside walls. Welding and high-strength bolting was used in constructing the walls, instead of riveting. High-strength steel plates were welded together to make box-shaped columns spaced every 3.33 feet (1.02 m) along the perimeter. The special, high-strength steel had strength triple that of the conventional steel used at the time the World Trade Center was built. The spandrel beams, or beams along outside walls, were 4.5 feet (1.4 m) deep. They were rigidly connected to the columns, so the walls would act nearly solid, with only small slots for windows. Engineers call this a perimeter tube frame. For fast construction, the walls came in panels 10 feet (3 m) wide and 36 feet (11 m) high, with three columns and three floors of beams already joined by welding. Even so, 5,828 such panels were needed, and the whole project required 200,000 separate pieces of steel. The panels weighed up to 20 tons (18 t) and were lifted into place by four Australian-made cranes. A new floor was built about every three days. Floor loads were carried on 28-inch-deep (71-cm-deep) steel trusses that reach from the perimeter to the core, or inside, columns. In the towers and basements, 192,000 tons (174,000 t) of steel supported 9 million square feet (836,000 m^2). That averages to 43 pounds of steel per square foot (210 kg/m^2) of floor.

The World Trade Center is shown here under construction. The red and white cranes are visible on the roof, as they construct the perimeter tube frame.

These fingers of steel are all that is left of the World Trade Center in the horrible aftermath of the September 11, 2001 terrorist attack.

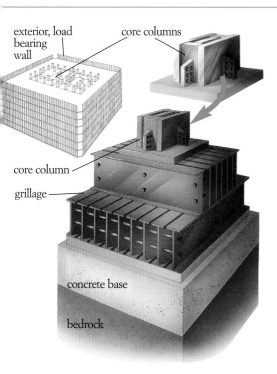

exterior, load bearing wall

core columns

core column

grillage

concrete base

bedrock

Above, top: A solid plate across each corner connects walls of closely spaced exterior columns to form a perimeter tube frame. Columns in the interior core are spaced farther apart.

Above, bottom: World Trade Center columns required thick steel plates at the bottom of the building. The load was spread from each column by a grillage, or criss-crossed beams, to bear on solid rock.

On September 11, 2001 the famous World Trade Center Towers were hit by a devastating terrorist attack. Two hijacked commercial airliners full of highly flammable jet fuel crashed into the towers and exploded. The tower structures were able to withstand the holes ripped in their sides and intense fires for an hour—long enough to allow many thousands of people to escape. Unfortunately, when the buildings finally collapsed there were still over 6,000 people trapped inside. We remember with sadness the lives lost. In remembering the greatness of these two famous skyscrapers and what they stood for we pay tribute to those who were lost.

The walls of Sears Tower step back at upper floors thanks to the use of nine bundled tubes of closely spaced columns.

walls step back

SEARS TOWER

New York is not the only place with famous skyscrapers. Sears Tower, in Chicago, is also a well-known member of the skyscraper family. It does not have walls that rise straight up on all sides, so it has a different frame than does the World Trade Center. In Sears Tower, steel columns are spaced 15 feet (4.6 m) apart. They outline nine squares, each 75 feet (22.9 m) on a side, like a tic-tac-toe game inside a square. Stiff beams were welded to the columns to create moment frames that act as bundled tubes, or a cellular tube frame. To complete the construction in three years, the steel frame was built in "trees" of 25-foot (7.6-m) columns with half-beams already rigidly attached. The four cranes lifted these columns, and then their ends were bolted together. In the finished building, 76,000 tons (69,000 t) of steel supports 4.1 million square feet (381,000 m²) of floor space, or only 35 pounds per square foot (171 kg/m²) of floor.

The Bank of China and the Jin Mao Tower

Right: Diagonal braces create a stiff, efficient truss to resist typhoon winds.

THE BANK OF CHINA

The Bank of China tower, in Hong Kong, has giant diagonal braces, or trusses, along its faces and through some floors to resist high wind forces from typhoons. Why use diagonals instead of moment frames? Think of a drinking straw. If you push it sideways, it is flexible and bends. However, if you pull or push on its ends, it is rather stiff. A jungle gym of moment frames is relatively flexible, as beams and columns bend. A trussed building frame, though, is like an old-fashioned steel bridge standing on end. The truss is much stiffer and each piece can be more efficient, using less steel. In this building, the frame has steel floor beams and diagonal trusses. However, the corner columns that carry vertical loads are mostly concrete, with thin, steel pieces included for connection purposes. The efficiency of the truss system, combined with the use of concrete, results in strength and stiffness with less steel tonnage. The 1.4 million square feet (130,000 m²) of floors are carried by 16,000 tons (14,515 t) of steel members and reinforcing bars, or just 23 pounds per square foot (112 kg/m²). That is impressive, since typhoon wind loads are twice those in New York City.

Right: An interesting shape resulted from stopping one quarter of the building floor plan at a time. The diagonals continue down through the floor space. I. M. Pei designed this unique building.

Jin Mao Tower

The designers of the Jin Mao Tower, in Shanghai, structure took an entirely different approach. Floors are supported on steel beams, but most of the frame is made with high-strength concrete. Concrete is widely used for building in China, so it made sense to use it for this building. Up through the center of the building, concrete walls create an octagonal tube, or eight-sided, that is a backbone or core about 90 feet (274 m) wide. The core's bottom 50 floors are filled with elevators, office bathrooms, and storage areas. Its upper 38 stories are empty, making a hotel atrium, or a large, open space. Steel truss arms, or outriggers, help the core resist overturning, or toppling, like ski poles help a skier to stand. The outriggers reach out from the core at floors 34, 51, and 87, and connect to steel buried within the two giant concrete "mega-columns" on each building face. Jin Mao's structure is called a core and outrigger system.

Right: The pagoda-like profile of Jin Mao reflects a design based on the Chinese lucky number 8. The lower half of the building has a large concrete core, shown shaded. In the upper half, the core is empty to create a hotel atrium with balconies.

The Petronas Towers

The Petronas Towers in Kuala Lumpur, Malaysia also rely mostly on concrete, but differ from the Jin Mao in significant ways. Winds in Malaysia are milder than either New York or Shanghai, which are on hurricane coastlines. Each tower has a central concrete core that is nearly square, about 75 feet (22.9 m) on each side. The core has concrete walls that range in thickness from 29.5 inches (75 cm) at lower floors to 13.8 inches (35 cm) at the top. However, the core can resist only half of the wind load. The rest of the wind load is resisted by a moment frame that forms a ring around the building. Sixteen concrete columns are connected by 3.7-foot-deep(1.15-m-deep) concrete beams. The beams are haunched, or thinner in the middle, to allow room for ceiling lights and air conditioning ducts. The columns are large, from 4 to 8 feet (1.2–2.4 m) in diameter. The concrete used has a crushing strength up to 11,600 pounds per square inch (8,143 t/m^2), triple the strength of typical concrete. This particular concrete was new to the area, but concrete construction is familiar in Malaysia so it was not a problem for the contractors.

Construction was completed in about three years, with as many as two floors being built per week. The core walls were built first, using three-story-high working platforms that were automated to climb on their own. The platforms allowed three different trades to work at the same time. Lathers, or reinforcing-bar (rebar) placers, tied on new rebar cages at the top level. Carpenters adjusted formwork and poured concrete at the middle level, and finishers smoothed off the three-day-old wall exposed at the bottom level. After the core was completed, perimeter columns and beams were set, or put in place. They looked like giant letter *T*s. Rebar was placed into the forms and concrete was pumped in. After three days, the forms were removed so floors could be placed. The floors were made of

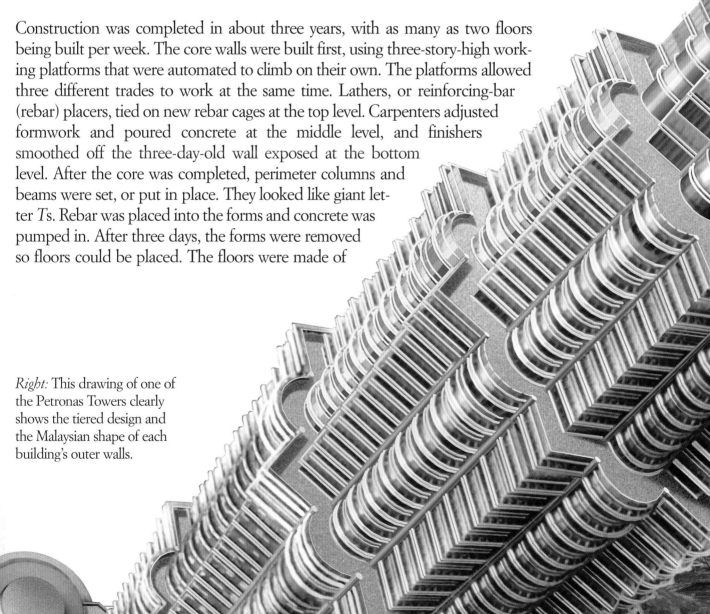

Right: The needle on each of the Petronas Towers has copper straps that direct electricity safely to the ground. Tall buildings are often struck by lightning. The straps ensure the safety of the people inside the building.

Right: This drawing of one of the Petronas Towers clearly shows the tiered design and the Malaysian shape of each building's outer walls.

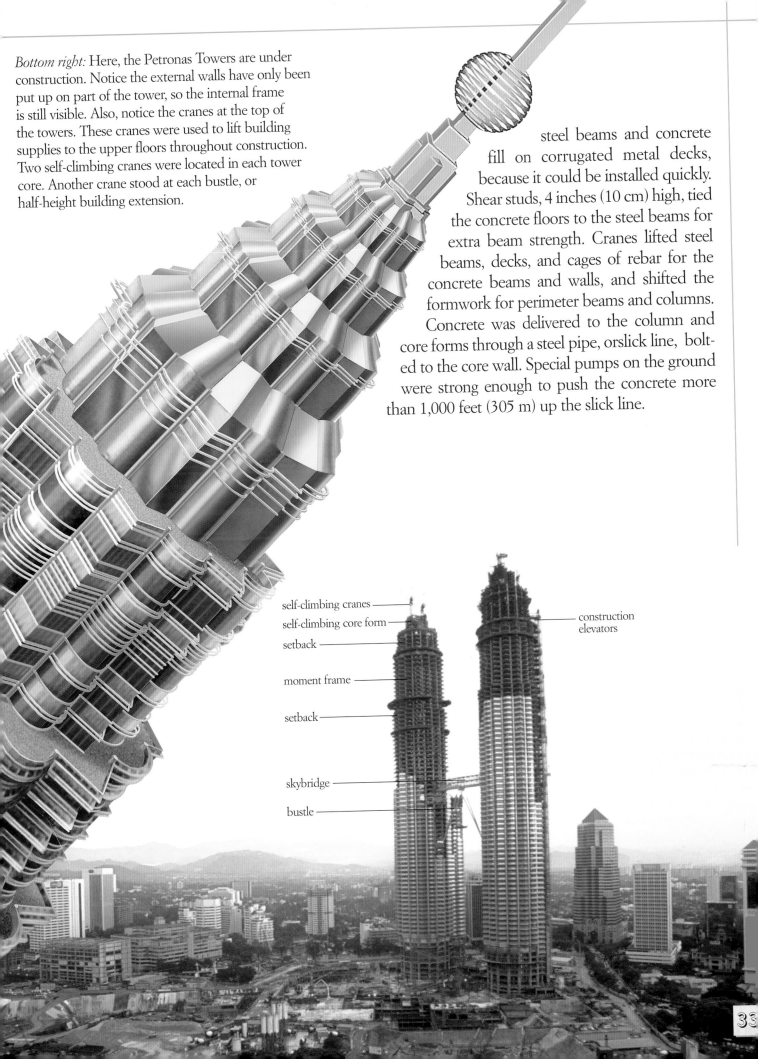

Bottom right: Here, the Petronas Towers are under construction. Notice the external walls have only been put up on part of the tower, so the internal frame is still visible. Also, notice the cranes at the top of the towers. These cranes were used to lift building supplies to the upper floors throughout construction. Two self-climbing cranes were located in each tower core. Another crane stood at each bustle, or half-height building extension.

steel beams and concrete fill on corrugated metal decks, because it could be installed quickly. Shear studs, 4 inches (10 cm) high, tied the concrete floors to the steel beams for extra beam strength. Cranes lifted steel beams, decks, and cages of rebar for the concrete beams and walls, and shifted the formwork for perimeter beams and columns. Concrete was delivered to the column and core forms through a steel pipe, orslick line, bolted to the core wall. Special pumps on the ground were strong enough to push the concrete more than 1,000 feet (305 m) up the slick line.

self-climbing cranes

self-climbing core form

setback

moment frame

setback

skybridge

bustle

construction elevators

A Tower Inside

Before the outside of the Petronas Towers could be completed, workers needed to install the floors. They used temporary construction elevators outside the building (see photo on page 32) to reach each level. As soon as the floors were laid, rails for permanent double-decked elevators were installed. The construction elevators were then removed, and the building exterior was completed. Next the interior was "fitted out." Interior designers, electricians, and other workers began to prepare the building for tenants. This process included installing the wiring for electicity and phones and the plumbing for bathrooms, as well as painting and creating an inviting interior.

Just as the outer structure is influenced by Malaysian and Islamic designs, so is the interior design. Stainless steel fittings and screens, which hang overhead, use designs inspired by carvings from villages along the east coast of Malaysia. Slatted screens are used to define spaces and to give a tranquil, cool interior despite the heat outside the towers.

Below, left: This cross-section of the elevator shafts at the center of one of the Petronas Towers shows how they fit between the large walls of the building's core. The core, or central rectangle, contains the various ducts and risers, or pipes, for HVAC, electricity, telephones, and other mechanical systems.

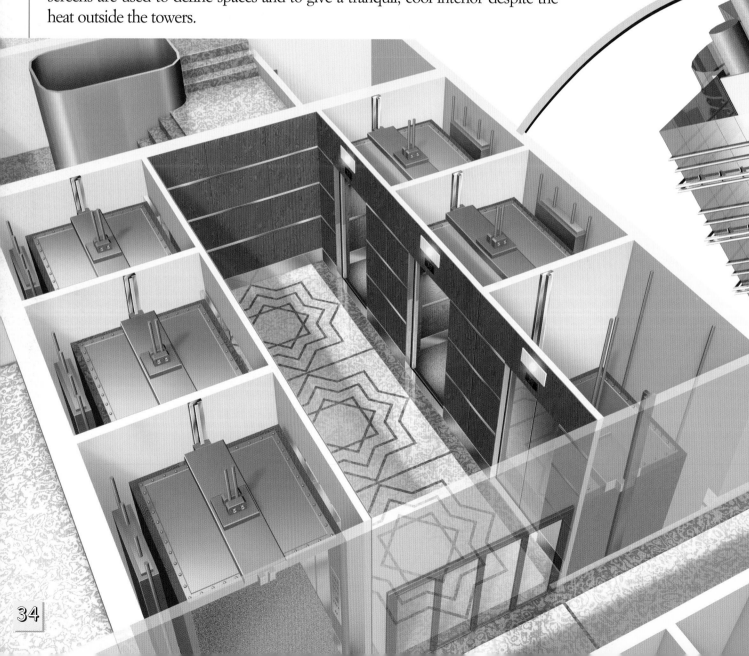

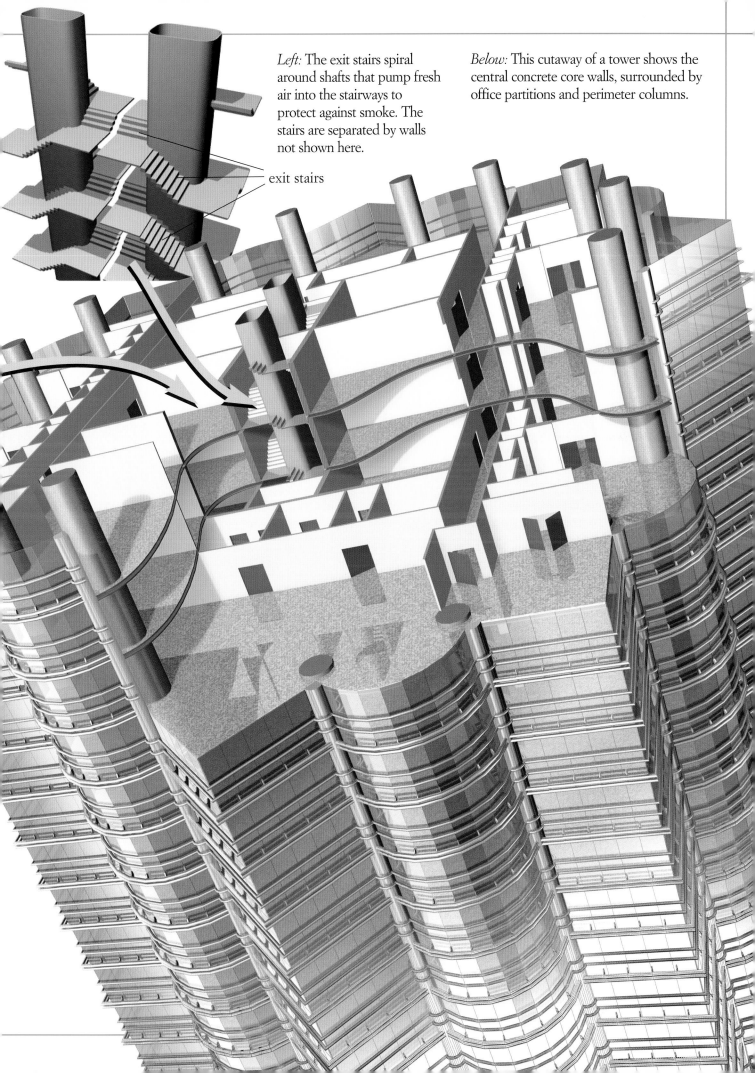

Left: The exit stairs spiral around shafts that pump fresh air into the stairways to protect against smoke. The stairs are separated by walls not shown here.

exit stairs

Below: This cutaway of a tower shows the central concrete core walls, surrounded by office partitions and perimeter columns.

The Bridge Between the Giants

A special challenge was the design and construction of the Skybridge, a double-deck bridge that crosses the 192-foot (58.5-m) gap between the towers. The glass-enclosed bridge allows people to cross between towers at the 41st and 42nd floors, 558 feet (170 m) in the air, to access offices and share conference rooms. It also serves as an emergency exit, so less space is needed for exit stairs at lower floors. The bridge walkway has slip connections and expansion joints, or floor gaps covered with sliding plates, at each tower. This allows the bridge to expand or contract with building movements. They can move as much as 1.3 feet (0.4 m) during a big storm, but likely movements are about half that. The walkway is carried on a simple arch, like an upside-down *V*, made with hollow steel pipes 3.7 feet (1.1 m) in diameter. Each leg rests on a Teflon pad at level 29 that slides over a stainless steel ball joint. The arch supports the middle of the bridge and keeps the walkway centered between the towers. The bridge was made in Korea. To install it, the lower portions of the arch legs were assembled first. Then, they were placed vertically on their bearings and tied to the towers. The upper legs were attached to the fully assembled bridge on the ground and lifted very slowly on eight high-strength cables. Lifting the 360-ton (325-t) bridge took three days. Finally, the legs were swung out and bolted to the walkway.

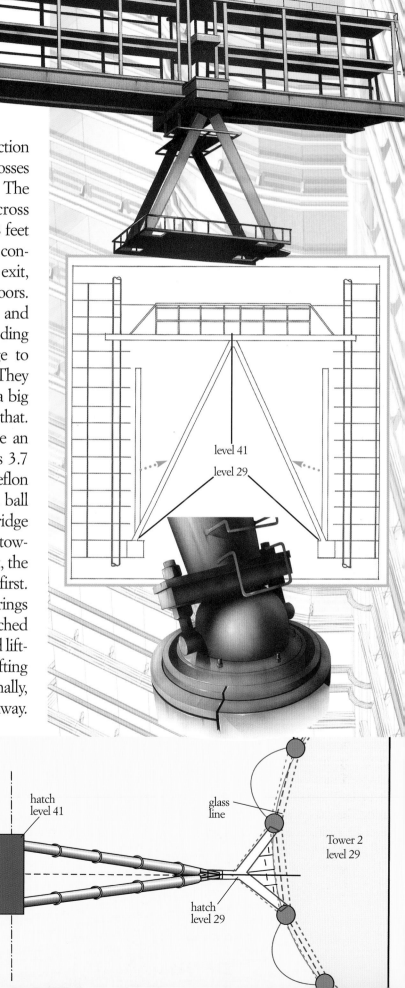

level 41

level 29

SKYBRIDGE LEG PLAN

hatch
level 29

hatch
level 41

glass
line

Tower 1
level 29

Tower 2
level 29

hatch
level 29

Facing page, top: The Skybridge was lifted in five large pieces. This is the largest piece. It included most of the bridge and the top 1/5 of each leg. It took 57 hours to lift into place using eight high-strength wires.

Facing page, second from top: The bridge legs were first laid against the towers. The last step in bridge erection was swinging them over and bolting them to the rest of the bridge.

Facing page, third from top: A ball joint at the bottom of each bridge leg allows movement as the towers sway in strong winds.

Facing page, bottom: The bridge spans the space between the two towers at levels 41 and 42. The bridge legs taper from level 41 and meet at the ball joints on level 29. This diagram shows where the legs attach to the towers.

The Petronas Towers and the Skybridge

A Vertical Town: The Hong Kong and Shanghai Bank

Not every tall building is a skyscraper, or a building that "makes the land pay." An owner with plenty of money may choose a unique building design for its special identity, even if it doesn't follow the usual real estate rules. The headquarters for the Hong Kong and Shanghai Bank, completed in 1985 in downtown Hong Kong, was said to be the world's most expensive office building (in dollars per square foot of floor area) at that time. At forty-eight stories, it's not one of the tallest buildings in town. It stands out anyway, thanks to a dramatic, exposed structural skeleton and special features, such as an open ground floor, a glass-bottomed central atrium, and sixty-two escalators.

This "vertical town" includes four groups of office floors, each with its own garden level, stacked on top of a glass-bottomed atrium. The banking hall and seven higher office floors line the atrium— just like buildings around a town square.

Norman Foster, the architect of the Hong Kong and Shanghai Bank building, used an indirect structural system, exposed for all to see. In it he emphasized the repetition of "modular" units in which premade elements were used. The floors are hung from tension rods that distribute building weight. The rods collect the load of several floors and are carried on the tips of triangular braces that project from each side of ladderlike towers. The towers distribute the load back to the ground. For wind, the towers work like eight flagpoles, anchored in the ground and are strengthened further by connecting braces that run between them.

The Hong Kong and Shanghai Bank's design is an excellent example of innovative, high-tech design, but is not really a skyscraper.

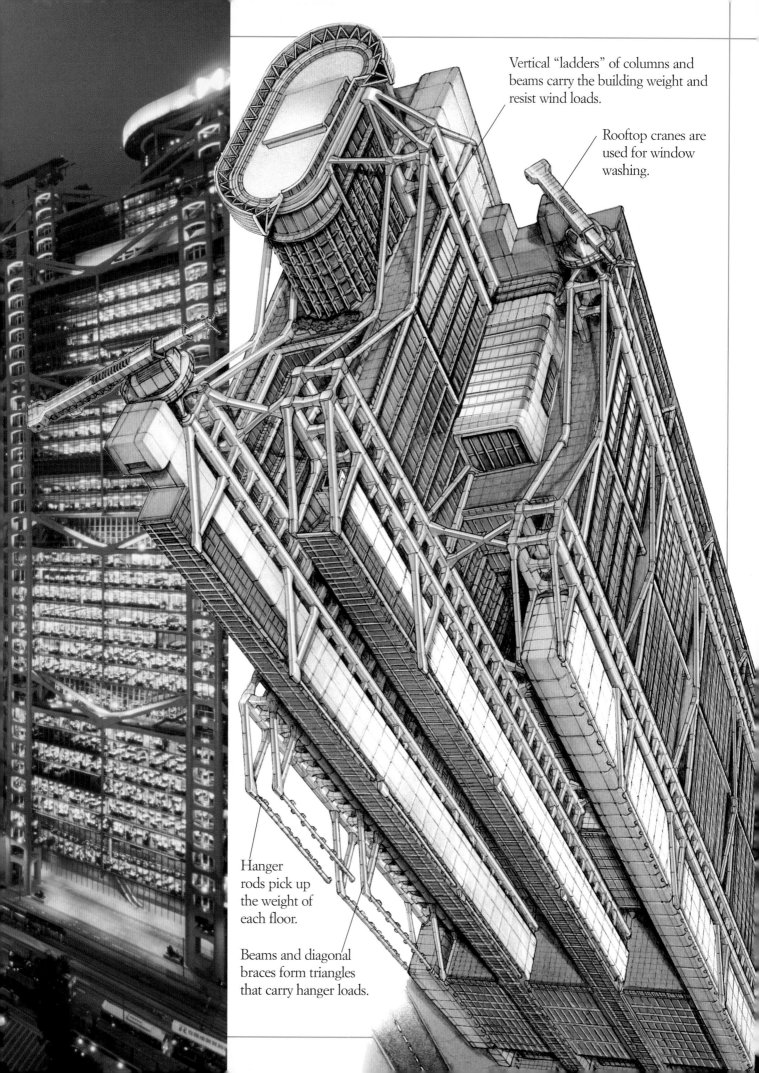

Vertical "ladders" of columns and beams carry the building weight and resist wind loads.

Rooftop cranes are used for window washing.

Hanger rods pick up the weight of each floor.

Beams and diagonal braces form triangles that carry hanger loads.

Mechanical Systems

A skyscraper without heating, ventilation, or air-onditioning would not be inviting to anyone. The system that provides these things is called an HVAC system. Different types of HVAC systems directly affect the architecture, structure, and building operations management, so the mechanical engineer, the architect, the structural engineer, and the owner must decide together on the best system.

Another mechanical system that can affect the people in the building is the elevator system. In extremely tall buildings, an efficient system is of huge importance. As buildings get taller, it is not practical to let every elevator stop at every floor. Some designers use banks, where elevators are grouped to serve certain floors, to solve the problem. For taller office buildings, elevators are usually grouped into banks serving sixteen floors or less. However, the higher elevators pass lower floors in express shafts that waste floor space. For the tallest skyscrapers, this waste is minimized by several strategies.

Skylobby floors allow local elevator shafts to be stacked over each other. At the ground floor lobby, people going to low floors enter a regular, local elevator that makes many stops. People going to high floors take a shuttle, or express, elevator from the ground floor to a skylobby. There they switch to a regular elevator that stops on their floor. Another strategy for reducing wasted space is the double-deck elevator cab. The cab has two floors that line up with two building floors at the same time, so twice as many people can travel in each elevator shaft. The Petronas Towers use both elevator strategies. They have a skylobby at level 41/42, and nearly all shuttle and local elevators are double-decked. This way only seventeen elevator shafts are needed to provide elevator service equivalent to forty-eight regular cabs.

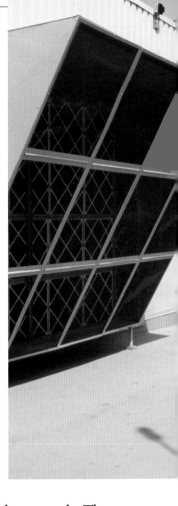

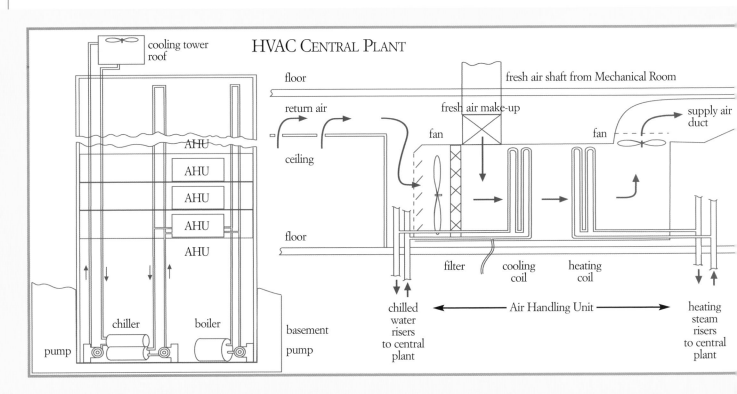

Above: This machine is part of an HVAC system. It pulls in fresh air through the vents.

Right: A diagram shows the different components of an elevator. There is a pully and counterweight in this example, which allow the elevator to move up and down. The pit has special braking mechanisms to make sure the elevator comes to a smooth stop.

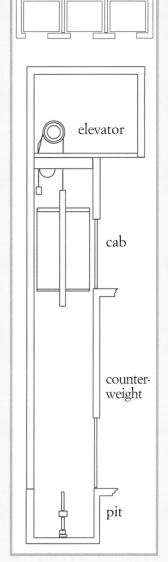

elevator

cab

counter-weight

pit

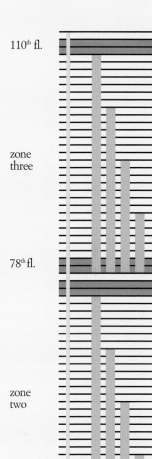

110th fl.

zone three

78th fl.

zone two

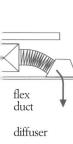

flex duct

diffuser

There are two main HVAC approaches for tall office buildings. Both use the same central plant. Centralized air distribution is a traditional system. Air from several floors is pulled through vertical return air shafts to mechanical rooms located 12 to 30 stories apart, where fresh air is mixed in. Giant fans then blow the air past heating and cooling coils and push it back through other shafts to supply the same floors. From the air supply shaft, air is distributed throughout each floor by air ducts, or long metal tubes. This approach was used at the World Trade Center.

Right: A schematic view of the World Trade Center's elevators shows how express and local runs are separated for maximum performance. Two different sets of huge shuttle elevators bring tenants directly to the 44th or 78th floor skylobbies. Four sets of local elevators then rise from each skylobby. Each bank only serves seven to ten floors.

1 Express to Top
2 Express to Skylobbies
3 Local Service
4 Skylobby Floors
5 Mechanical Floors

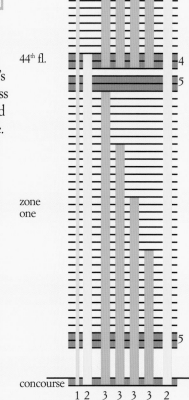

44th fl.

zone one

concourse

1 2 3 3 3 3 2

The Future

Right now, the Petronas Towers are officially the world's tallest buildings, standing 1,483 feet (452 m) measured to their structural tops. Sears Tower holds the category of tallest building antenna, 1,730 feet (527.3 m). That's because the CN Tower in Toronto, 1,815 feet (553.3 m) tall, is considered a broadcast and observation tower, not a skyscraper building. Sears Tower also has the highest roof, at 1,450 feet (442 m) and the highest occupied floor, at 1,431 feet (436.2 m). New record-breaking projects are being proposed, and some are started, all the time.

The Taipei Financial Center in Taiwan is under construction, with a planned height of 1,666 feet (507.8 m) to the structural top when completed in 2003. In addition to remarkably fast observation elevators, this steel-framed tower with concrete-filled supercolumns includes a tuned mass damper and double-notched building corners that reduce wind motion for occupant comfort. It also uses the Chinese lucky-eight theme, including eight tapering blocks of eight floors each in its one hundred and one stories.

The Shanghai Financial Center, a modernistic, wedge-shaped building with a hole through the top, began construction as a ninety-story, 1,518-foot (462.7 m) project. Due to financial conditions, construction was halted. However, developer Mori plans a redesign to increase the height when it begins again.

1. 1,620-foot (494-m) San Paolo Tower Project, San Paolo, Brazil.

2. 1,666-foot (508-m) Financial Center, Taipei, Taiwan.

3. 2,756-foot (840-m) Millennium Tower, Tokyo, Japan.

A 5.4-million-square-foot tower that is 1,914 feet (583.6 m) tall is also being designed for Kowloon, across the harbor from Hong Kong, and a tower standing 1,280 feet (390.1 m) tall has been proposed for London.

These projects are all slender towers. However, a giant pyramid was proposed for San Paolo, Brazil. It has not gone ahead into construction. Giant, bulky projects pose several interesting design challenges. First, the floors will be enormous, so most occupants would not be near a window. Will people want to live or work in a skyscraper if they never see the views?

A three-dimensional rendering of the Shanghai skyline with the World Financial Center now in construction in the foreground. Jin Mao is just to its right.

Second, the occupancy could be several times greater than in any building to date. Is it practical to move around in such a building? The Odyssey transportation system developed by Otis Elevator Co. in 1996 uses individually-powered and computer-guided "pods" to climb up and down shafts and across floors, like little trains spaced along the same tracks. A similar technology has been used for years to distribute mail within buildings. This eliminates the space wasted by one elevator in a long shaft, but requires the confidence of the public in trusting that the technology will work.

Third, developers expect that people would live and work in the same building, so street access and commuter services would be less important. Is this what people want? What happens when people change jobs and must start commuting? Fourth, how will air supply and fire protection be handled, when so much of the building is so far from the outdoors?

It is certain that such giant projects will eventually be built, if developers and bankers think the projects can be profitable. Their effect on the residents, on neighbors, and on entire cities will be fascinating to watch.

Skyscrapers were developed as "machines that make the land pay." This book shows how the "machines" work, from the people in crowded cities willing to pay the rent, to the inventions that made it practical to work and live in such tall buildings. The question now is, "Will people still want and need skyscrapers?" It costs more to build tall. Will some people always be willing to pay more to live or work up high? Will people choose to live outside cities and telecommute instead? For now, skyscrapers are still going up. Nobody knows what new developments tomorrow might bring.

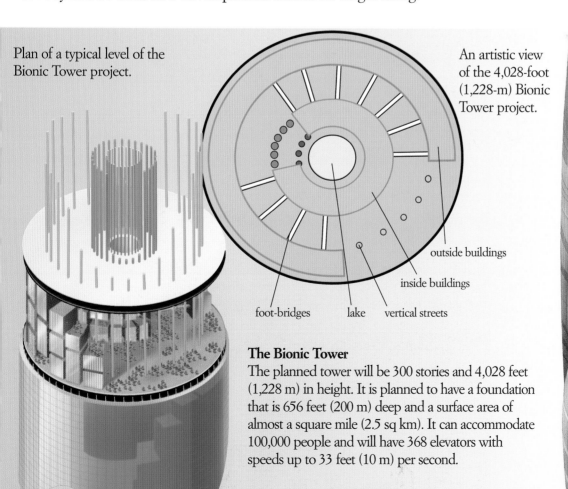

Plan of a typical level of the Bionic Tower project.

An artistic view of the 4,028-foot (1,228-m) Bionic Tower project.

foot-bridges lake vertical streets

inside buildings

outside buildings

The Bionic Tower
The planned tower will be 300 stories and 4,028 feet (1,228 m) in height. It is planned to have a foundation that is 656 feet (200 m) deep and a surface area of almost a square mile (2.5 sq km). It can accommodate 100,000 people and will have 368 elevators with speeds up to 33 feet (10 m) per second.

Glossary

aeroelastic (air-oh-ee-LAS-tic) Having the ability to sway in the wind.

aeronautical (ayr-oh-NAW-tih-kul) Having to do with the science of flight.

air duct (AIR DUKT) A horizontal sheet metal tube found in a building.

air handling unit (AIR HAND-ling YOO-niht) A fan, with heating and cooling coils, in a box.

air shaft (AIR SHAFT) A tall, narrow tube that provides air to building floors.

altitude (AL-tih-tood) The height above the ground, or how tall it reaches.

atrium (AY-tree-uhm) A courtyard found in the middle of a building.

barrette (bah-RET) A concrete-filled rectangular pier.

beam (BEEM) A horizontal member between two supports.

bustle (BUS-sel) A shorter, secondary tower connected to a main tower at all floors.

cement (seh-MEHNT) Powder made of burned clay and limestone.

column (KAH-luhm) A vertical member carrying vertical compression load.

compression (cum-PREH-shun) The direction of force that squeezes a member.

concrete (KON-kreet) A mixture of cement, sand, gravel, and water.

core (KOR) The central portion of a building, including stairs.

curtain wall (KUR-tin WOL) Exterior wall that hangs from a building frame.

damper (DAM-pur) A device to reduce vibration movement.

debris (duh-BREE) Broken pieces of a building.

developer (dee-VEH-luh-pur) One who organizes new construction.

erect (ee-REKT) To assemble building pieces in a final location.

excavation (ek-ska-VAY-shun) The removal of soil to create a hole or hollow.

expansion joint (ek-SPAN-shun JOYNT) A gap in a structure to allow movement of parts.

expertise (ek-sper-TEES) Specialized skill or knowledge in a field.

FAR (Floor Area Ratio) The usable floor space in a building divided by the area of land on which the building stands.

fabricate (FA-brih-kayt) To construct something or to assemble from parts.

fire-rated (FYR-rayt-ed) Having a known, tested ability to hold fire back.

fluorescent light (flaw-RES-ent LYT) The light from long, glowing white tubes.

formwork (FORM-wurk) Walls or containers used to hold wet concrete.

foundation mat (fown-DAY-shun MAT) Thick reinforced concrete below the basement, slightly longer and wider than the building footprint, that spreads building weight from columns and walls out onto soil, piles, or barrettes below.

grade (GRAYD) The elevation, or level, of the ground before building begins.

grillage (GRIL-ihj) Crisscrossed, short beams used to spread load.

haunched (HAWNCHT) Varying in depth so it is thicker at the ends.

HVAC (AYCH-VEE-AY-SEE) Heating, ventilating, and air conditioning systems within a building.

lateral loads (LAT-uh-rul LOHDZ) Sideways forces, like wind and earthquakes, that a building or structure must withstand.

load-bearing (LOHD-bair-ing) Walls, or structures that carry vertical forces, like building weight.

massing (MAS-sing) An architectural term for overall building shape.

master board (MAS-ter BORD) The central location where controls are located.

modular (MAH-dyu-ler) Built of multiple, identical or similar pieces.

moment (MOH-ment) The bending force in a beam or column.

moment frame (MOH-ment FRAYM) Beams and columns rigidly joined together to resist moments in the beams by moments in the columns.

negotiation (neh-go-she-AY-shun) A discussion between people who are trying to reach an agreement.

outrigger (OWT-rih-ger) A piece that sticks out from a main structure to provide additional stability or support.

parcel (PAR-suhl) The real estate term for a small portion of land.

partition (par-TIH-shun) A non-load-bearing wall separating spaces.

perimeter (puh-RIH-meh-ter) The boundary of a closed figure, in this case refers to the frame of a building.

perimeter supporting column (puh-RIH-meh-ter sup-POR-ting CAH-lum) A post, located just behind the exterior wall, that carries the weight of the wall and the floor nearby.

pier (PEER) A column buried in soil or rock for foundation.

pile (PYL) A long, slender column, usually made of wood, steel, or reinforced concrete, that is driven into the ground to carry a vertical load.

prefabricated (pree-FA-brih-kayt-ed) Made at a factory so construction consists of assembling standardized parts.

ravine (ruh-VEEN) A deep and narrow valley.

rebar (REE-bahr) A steel reinforcing bar or rod used in concrete.

reinforced concrete (re-in-FORSD KON-kreet) Concrete with embedded steel rods to make it stronger.

riser (RY-zer) A vertical, mechanical pipe.

rivet (RIH-vet) A steel fastener with two rounded heads used to join pieces of steel. Replaced today by bolts, which are easier to use.

salvage (SAL-vij) Property or material saved or rescued which is believed to have value.

savanna (suh-VA-nuh) A plain of coarse grasses and scattered trees.

scaffolding (SKA-ful-ding) A temporary structure or platform that is built over a sidewalk or other area, to protect the public as well as to provide a work space for construction on a building.

setback (SET-bak) The term used when wall face is shifted back, like layers on a wedding cake.

shear (SHEER) An action or a stress caused by a force that tries to make one part slide sideways over another part.

shock absorber (SHOK AB-zorb-er) A piston-in-cylinder machine used to absorb energy.

silt (SIHLT) A type of soil that has a particle size, or consistency, between that of clay and sand.

slurry (SLER-ee) A flowing mixture of water and soil.

slurry wall (SLER-ee WAHL) A special wall built to make foundations watertight.

span (SPAN) The distance between beam supports

spandrel beam (SPAYN-drehl BEEM) A beam along the outside wall of a building.

subcontractor (sub-KON-trak-ter) A person or business that is hired to perform work under another person or business's contract.

sway (SWAY) The lateral movement at the top of a building.

tension (TEN-shyun) The direction of force that stretches a member.

tieback (TY-bak) A strong wire used to hold basement walls against soil until floors can be constructed to hold back the walls.

tongue and groove (TUNG AND GROOV) A joint made by a tongue or an edge on one board sliding into a groove or an indentation on another board.

tremie (TREM-ee) The method of placing concrete underwater.

truss (TRUHS) A frame formed by members arranged in triangles.

turbulence (TUR-byu-lens) Wind irregularities like gusts and lulls.

typhoon (ty-FOON) A powerful, cyclonic storm, like a hurricane, that occurs in East Asia.

weathering (WEH-thuh-ring) The weakening of something, like a building, by exposure to sun, rain, and frost.

wind tunnel (WIND TUH-nuhl) A long, narrow room with air pushed by fans to simulate forces exerted on buildings or other things.

X-brace (EKS-brays) Diagonal member pairs used for frame stiffening.

yield strength (YEELD STRENKTH) Force used when steel begins to stretch like taffy.

Additional Resources

To learn more about skyscrapers, check out the following books and Web sites.

Books

Darling, David. *Spiderwebs to Skyscrapers—the Science of Structures*. Dillon Press: New York, 1991.

Severanace, John B. S*kyscrapers, How America Grew Up*. Holiday House: New York, 2000.

Wilcox, Charlotte. *A Skyscraper Story*. Carolrhoda Books: Minneapolis, MN, 1990.

Web Sites

www.ctbuh.org
www.greatbuildings.com/buildings
www.historychannel.com/exhibits/skyscrapers

Index

About the Author

Leonard M. Joseph ("Len") knows skyscrapers inside and out from personal experience. As a senior vice president and principal (part owner) at Thornton-Tomasetti Engineers in New York City, he has spent the last twenty-five years designing structural frames for buildings, including five years working on the Petronas Towers team. To prepare for this work, Len received a Bachelor of Science degree from Cornell University in New York, and Master of Science and Master of Business Administration degrees from Stanford University in California. He then registered as a professional engineer in New York and a structural engineer in California. His other designs include hangars for military jets, San Francisco's baseball stadium Pacific Bell Park, Boston pedestrian bridges, and the skyscrapers One Mellon Bank Center in Pittsburgh, Pennsylvania, and Chifley Tower in Sydney, Australia. He has also investigated the Hartford Civic Center Coliseum collapse and the Schoharie Creek Bridge failure. Len lives near New York City with his wife and son. He continues to work on buildings from New York to Taiwan, and he enjoys sharing lessons in design and construction through talks and books.

Photo Credits